ONE-ROOM SCHOOL

by Raymond Bial

HOUGHTON MIFFLIN COMPANY
Boston 1999

"It's almost time for the bell, Ida said, and they all turned back to the schoolhouse. They must not be late. In the entry they drank from the dipper that floated in the water pail there. Then they went in, tanned and windblown, and hot and dusty."

—Laura Ingalls Wilder, *Little Town on the Prairie*

ONE-ROOM SCHOOLHOUSES

once dotted the American landscape from the Atlantic seaboard to the Pacific shores. For nearly 250 years — from the 1700s to the 1950s — more than seven generations of children were educated in these little schools. Among the students were George Washington, Abraham Lincoln, and Laura Ingalls Wilder.

Today, only a few one-room schoolhouses remain, abandoned at rural crossroads or standing alone in pastures. The desks, benches, and potbelly stoves are gone — sold at auction years ago. Outside, there may be a hand

School names reflected people's love of place and hope in the future: some schools were called Harmony, Apple Pie, and Good Intent, as well as Poison Spider and Bellyache School. Others were called Prairie Rose, Fairview, Possum Hollow, Buzzard Roost, and Frog Pond.

pump, now orange with rust, a pair of teetering outhouses, and the traces of a ball field, though wildflowers and streaming grasses have probably reclaimed the yard. Yet the schools have not been forgotten. Hundreds of personal reminiscences written by students and teachers recount the joys of school days. Their clear-eyed affection makes one wonder what was so special about these schools. Why did this effective means of educating young people come to be replaced by large schools with hundreds, often thousands, of students? What can we learn from the experiences of the past?

At one time there were no schools in America. Colonial children from well-to-do families were taught at home; others received no formal instruction. Gradually, subscription schools in which parents paid an enrollment fee were started. The colony of Massachusetts established the first public schools in 1647 so "that learning may not be buried in the graves of our fathers." Schoolmasters taught reading, writing, and arithmetic, but their emphasis was upon religious instruction and Latin.

Thomas Jefferson believed that public education was essential to the survival of democracy in the young republic of the United States. People had to be well educated if they were going to vote intelligently, serve on juries, and assume other civic duties. Jefferson assured that the future states of Ohio, Illinois, Indiana, Wisconsin, and Michigan would have land set aside for public schools. "Religion, morality, and knowledge," stated the Northwest Ordinance of 1787, which created this region, "being necessary to good government, and the happiness of mankind, schools, and the means of education, shall forever be preserved."

By the 1830s, public schools had largely replaced private instruction in the bustling cities of the East. However, on the expanding frontier, from Ohio to Oregon, homesteaders put up their own schoolhouses—log cabins in the woods, soddies and dugouts on the broad, treeless prairies, and adobe buildings in the deserts. Sessions in these early schoolhouses lasted only a few months each year. Either a traveling schoolmaster or a local widow assumed responsibility for teaching the students. These schools had few, if any, books. Scholars, as students were then called, learned their lessons by reciting them

Early leaders recognized the importance of education. George Washington attended a country school. In turn, patriotic pictures of Washington and Lincoln, along with historic events, adorned the schoolhouse walls.

Log schools were constructed without nails because iron was scarce. In 1884 people built the last log cabin school in Missouri, quite similar to this one. As late as 1887, a cabin was used for a school in a lumber camp in Michigan.

out loud in what came to be known as "blab schools." Here's one popular rhyme that pioneer children recited in class to learn multiplication:

Twice times one is two.

This book is nearly new.

Twice times two is four.

Lay it on the floor.

Twice times three is six.

We're always playing tricks.

Twice times four is eight.

The books are always late.

Twice times five is ten.

Let's do it all again!

Abraham Lincoln attended classes for only a few weeks at a time and received his formal education "by littles" in blab schools. He and his sister, Sarah, walked two miles to a log school with a dirt floor in Kentucky. Later, dressed in a raccoon cap, moccasins, and buckskin clothes, he went to a log school in the woods of Indiana. The future president became the best speller in school and, at home, he did all the writing for his family. He ciphered, or solved math problems, on a wooden board, then shaved the numbers off with a knife for the next lesson.

Log schools were furnished with puncheon benches — split logs with legs pegged into the rounded underside. Hard and uncomfortable, they also had no backrests, so students had to sit up straight all day long.

The schoolmaster ruled the one-room cabin from behind a sturdy desk warmed by the fireplace and illumined by candlelight. His supplies included a copy of the Bible and a switch (a slender tree branch) for disciplining unruly students.

The first schoolhouses were made of prairie sod, logs, and adobe (bricks made of straw and clay). Out on the prairie there were few trees and people made "soddies" out of the land itself. Here a group of students and their teacher stand outside their Kansas school in the mid-1800s.

Early schools flourished because parents yearned for their children to receive a good education. James Rooney, a former student of a one-room school in Texas, observed, "It seemed, as I recall it, a lonely little house of scholarship, with its playground worn so bare that even the months of sun and idleness failed to bring any grass. But that humble little school had a dignity of a fixed and far-off purpose. . . . It was the outpost of civilization. It was the advance guard of the pioneer, driving the wilderness farther to the west. It was life preparing wistfully for the future."

By the mid-1800s, schools came to be established in districts small enough

that every child could walk to school. Members of local school boards were elected. They discussed and decided the school's location at a county crossroads or on an acre of land donated by a local farmer, usually in the center of the district. Communities began to construct sturdy wood-frame, brick, or stone buildings instead of log cabins and soddies. Most schools were wood-frame buildings of a vernacular, or native, design. Standardized schoolhouses, based on plan books, did not become common until after about 1910. If the location of these small buildings proved unsuitable, they could simply be placed on skids and pulled by teams of horses to another site.

Some schools were dugouts—holes literally scraped out of a hillside. Here a class from the mid-1800s stands in front of their Kansas school. These schools were replaced, often years later, with neat wood-frame buildings.

People were as devoted to their school district as they were to their farms and small businesses. Most often, they arranged for a highly skilled carpenter to erect a wood-frame school building, although there were also brick and stone schoolhouses.

Whatever their design, the buildings had just one room because the school had to be managed by a single teacher. The rooms varied in size but were always small enough that the teacher's voice could carry to the farthest corner. Most had a cloakroom at the entrance with hooks or nails for coats and hats and a shelf for lunch pails. A lower shelf held a washbasin along with a bar of homemade soap and a cotton towel. Furnishings included blackboards, desks, and benches. The front row of seats usually didn't have desktops; the students sat here during recitations. There was also the teacher's desk and a potbelly stove.

Girls sat on one side of the schoolroom and boys on the other. Children who misbehaved had to sit on the opposite side—a punishment that sometimes backfired. One boy recalled being sent to the girls' side to sit right behind his beloved Martha.

The school board chose the textbooks and hired the teacher who would be responsible for the district's children. These rugged farmers with calloused hands were often unschooled themselves, yet they respected education. A few communities neglected their schools; they had rattletrap desks on warped floors and few supplies. Yet most board members dutifully managed their schools, and the schools belonged to everyone in their communities. Appalachian author Jesse Stuart wrote of his father, who served on the board: "There wasn't anything within his power he wouldn't do for the Plum Grove School."

By the mid-1800s, the school year was divided into summer and winter terms. Most farm boys who needed to help with planting and harvesting at home attended only the winter session, from mid-November to mid-April. After 1900, schools offered just one term of about eight months.

Students enjoyed walking, riding on horseback over the open prairies, or taking a horse and buggy to school. As one former student recalled, "The road to school was wonderful; rich in color in autumn and tuneful with frogs in the spring." In the clear light of October and among the sweet blossoms of April, children came upon rabbits, muskrats, field mice, gophers, and skunks. They waded through wildflowers—black-eyed Susans, sweet Williams, and purple coneflowers—and bluestem grasses, or they followed a woodland path. Yet students also faced blizzards, tornadoes, thunderstorms, and long, gray days of drizzle. One student recalled, "I remember when it snowed so bad, it was so deep we'd walk on the snowbank clear above the fences." The weather could also be unpredictable—boys might change into itchy woolen long underwear on a chilly autumn morning only to have the day turn unseasonably warm. Or children might leave their coats at home only to have an April snowstorm descend upon them on their way home in the afternoon.

Bell towers were expensive and many school districts could not afford them. In a lot of schools, teachers stood in the doorway or in the schoolyard and rang a hand bell to call their students to class.

Schools were usually heated by a potbelly stove fed with coal, split wood, or corn cobs. It was placed in the center or at one end of the room so that students froze in the corners of the room and roasted near the stove. One student called it "the black monster."

Generally, school was held from eight o'clock in the morning to four o'clock in the afternoon. When the teacher clanged the hand bell or pulled the rope on the bell in the tower, the students formed two lines—one of girls and one of boys. First the girls and then the boys entered the school and stood by their desks. The teacher greeted the students and then, as one former pupil recounted, "We always opened the morning either by giving the Pledge of Allegiance or singing 'The Star Spangled Banner' or 'My Country, 'Tis of Thee.'" Then students dug into their morning assignments, studying in textbooks and writing on slates. As the students worked, the teacher walked about the room, checking their progress; she also called small groups to the front of the room to recite their lessons.

Students ranged in age from four-year-olds to rowdy farm boys as old as eighteen. Teachers worked hard, preparing as many as forty lesson plans each day for the thirty or more students who were grouped by their level of academic progress. But teachers had many helpers in their classes. Older students took pride in tutoring younger classmates in reading, ciphering (arithmetic), and other subjects. Recalling an especially bright student, a South Dakota teacher said, "I had to hustle to keep her busy and challenged." So she asked the girl to teach the younger students who needed help. "She loved it. So did I. And everyone profited from it. Of course, she did not get paid. But she got a better education."

There were usually three recesses: morning, noon, and afternoon. Mid-morning, the students were allowed to "turn out" for outhouse privileges, followed by a brief recess. One student recalled, "If it was cold, there wasn't much difficulty keeping them in the schoolroom; but if it was a nice day, everybody had to go out." Students returned to the school for more lessons, and at noon they had an hour for lunch and recess. "I remember we took our tin

Noon recess meant home-cooked meals toted in sturdy metal buckets—sandwiches of cold sliced meat, dill pickles, hard-boiled eggs, and perhaps a jar of potato salad. Students washed down their lunch with water drawn from a well or nearby spring.

lunch buckets to the cobhouse and crawled up on the pile of cobs in the back to eat our lunches," said Anna Williams, who attended Mr. Snip School in Illinois. "I can still remember the stuffed green peppers with their lids pinned on with toothpicks that Leota Wienke often had in her lunch." For dessert they might have a wedge of homemade pie or a hunk of gooey chocolate cake wrapped in waxed paper. With the bounty of good food, there was often a lot of swapping among the students. Less fortunate students might have only two slices of bread smeared with lard to make a sandwich and little else to offer in trade. After lunch, students hauled firewood or water back into the schoolhouse; then they were free to play.

Everyone shared a washbasin, soap, and towels placed in the cloakroom at the entrance to the school. Here they washed up for lunch and after playing in the dirt of the schoolyard at recess.

The carpenter might also be asked to construct outhouses—one for the girls and one for the boys—and perhaps a woodshed to store fuel for the potbelly stove that would heat the school through the long winter.

McGuffey Readers became the most influential set of books in American education. Written in the 1830s by William McGuffey, an Ohio professor, these books were ideally suited to the times and the needs of the people. Living in the rural countryside, with no theaters or libraries, the books became a sampler of the best of world literature. Instead of moving to the next grade, students advanced to the next McGuffey Reader, which went from a primer through a sixth volume.

Here is the first stanza of a poem from *McGuffey's Fourth Eclectic Reader* that students across the country once committed to memory:

From the pages of the McGuffey's Readers, Iowa novelist Hamlin Garland learned to "love the poems of Scott, Byron, Southey, Wordsworth, and a long line of English masters." He also got his first taste of Shakespeare from the books.

Try, Try Again
'Tis a lesson you should heed,
Try, try again;
If at first you don't succeed,
Try, try again;
Then your courage should appear,
For, if you persevere,
You will conquer, never fear;
Try, try again.

The first scratchy blackboards were pine boards painted with a mixture of egg white and carbon from charred potatoes. Teachers and students wrote with lumps of chalk, called crayons, and wiped down the board with rags.

Most of the lessons from these books took the form of memorization of poems, essays, and orations. Every day students were required to learn a verse, new spelling words, the names of the United States presidents, the state capitals, and other facts. The schoolday was varied—students worked at the blackboard parsing sentences, breaking them down and explaining the part of speech and function of every word. Learning through drills, memory, and recitation, students seldom had difficulty moving to high schools because they were so familiar with the basic subjects. One student likened his memory to a sturdy horse. The more he asked of it, within reasonable limits, the better it performed.

To liven up the day, teachers often had students go to the blackboard to see who could solve an arithmetic problem first. Students looked forward to this

When slate chalkboards became available and affordable, teachers used them, along with cylinders of white chalk and felt erasers. Students often helped by wiping down the blackboard and clapping the erasers together out in the schoolyard.

keen competition. One young man described a fellow classmate readying himself, "He would crouch with one foot braced against the blackboard wall and the other well back, his eyes like slits, his eraser hand poised as his chalk hand moved up one column and down the next." Or the teacher might ask students to solve problems in their heads: Take two, add two, add six, add ninety-eight, subtract eight, divide by ten, multiply by ten, add ten, and how many have you?

On Friday afternoons, or at the end of each day, students participated in "spelldowns." They stood in a line and spelled out the words they had diligently memorized. If a student missed a word and the next person got it right, she moved ahead in the line. The student standing at the head of the line when time ran out received the "head mark" for the day. Many students proudly remembered the number of head marks they won over the years.

Discipline was essential to learning in one-room schools. As early as the 1700s, Benjamin Franklin had advised in his almanac, "Discipline in the classroom is as necessary as discipline on the highway." Drawn from the word

Under the watchful eye of their teacher, these students at Morton School near Groton, New York, were called to the blackboard to solve arithmetic problems in 1907.

Teachers were quick to discipline students and they were supported by parents, who were disgraced if their children misbehaved. Order was believed to be necessary for learning and the instruments of discipline included hickory switches and dunce caps.

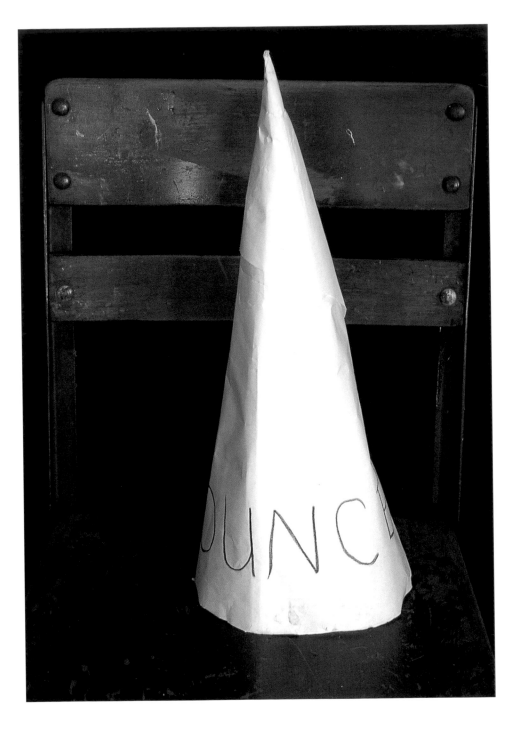

"disciple," meaning one who receives instruction from another, discipline was primarily a means of keeping order. Some students complained that teachers went through whole groves of hickory sticks in punishing them for the slightest infractions. However, if students were treated justly, they respected their teachers and the necessity of discipline to their own personal growth. Discipline was part of students' home life as well. Back on the farm, cows had to be milked, crops needed to be tended, eggs needed to be collected, and livestock had to be fed and watered day in and day out. Young people carried these work habits into the schoolroom and on through their adult lives.

Brandishing a hickory switch as long as she is tall, this no-nonsense schoolmarm at the Early American Museum in Mahomet, Illinois, explains its use to a contemporary audience of young people and their parents.

School lessons emphasized virtues as well, including honesty, diligence, and good habits. The McGuffey Readers imparted lessons such as this whimsical verse against smoking:

> Tobacco is a filthy weed,
> It was the Devil sowed the seed,
> It leaves a stench whe'er it goes,
> It makes a chimney of the nose.

Around the classroom were displayed inspirational sayings: What You Are to Be, You Are Now Becoming; Live to Learn—Strive to Excel; Do Your Best; and Be Kind and Courteous. One school in Greenwood County, Kansas, was even named Know Thyself, from a snippet of Alexander Pope's *Essay on Man,* published in a reader. There were plenty of school rules as well: respect God, parents, and the teacher; get along with schoolmates; strive to be quiet and not disturb the class. After recess, students were admonished: "Wash your hands and face. If you are barefoot, wash your feet."

Older boys, who often didn't want to be in school, sometimes attempted to "get" the teacher, whom they considered to be their arch enemy. They might "smoke the teacher out" by climbing on the roof of the school and blocking the chimney with a board. When he fled the smoky room, they pelted him with snowballs or challenged him to a fistfight. Often, school boards hired a male teacher during the winter session in hopes that he could better handle the older boys. However, well-known educator Horace Mann preferred women as

Whether they tutored other students or not, over the course of their education students repeated every lesson many times—they watched older students work out arithmetic problems at the blackboard and later studied the lessons themselves.

teachers: "Their manners are more mild and gentle, and hence in consonance with the tenderness of childhood." Teaching was considered one of the few "respectable" jobs for women, and by the 1890s, there were more school-marms than schoolmasters, although women were not allowed to teach after they married. Many teachers were as young as sixteen, but they rose to the occasion, especially when danger threatened—no matter whether it came from weather or animals. One teacher calmly disposed of a rattlesnake that a prankster had placed in her desk drawer. As a parent on the Western frontier

The smoke rising from the chimney of a log cabin school often tempted vengeful older boys who wished to get even with the schoolmaster, especially if one of them had been the victim of an unfair or embarrassing punishment.

stated, "If a teacher hasn't enough sense and know-how to kill a snake, she had better go back where she came from. It is twenty miles to the closest doctor, and death would arrive first." When she was hired as a teacher Laura Ingalls Wilder recounted her anxious feelings in *Little Town on the Prairie*, "She could not think what it would be to teach school twelve miles away from home, alone among strangers. She did not want to think about it. She did not want to go. The less she thought of it the better, for she must go, and she must meet whatever happened as it came."

Along with their meager pay, the only "benefits" teachers received were promises to keep the school building in good repair and to supply fuel for the potbelly stove. Teachers also did the janitorial work—sweeping, mopping, and wiping down blackboards. They toted water and hauled firewood or coal, arriving early to get a fire going before the children came to school. The wise teacher knew to incorporate some of this manual work into her discipline program.

Although paid very little, teachers had many other duties as well. They lugged coal in buckets like this one and kept a fire burning in the potbelly stove. They maintained the building and treated sick or injured children under their care.

Not only students but teachers had to adhere to strict rules of good behavior. Here are some guidelines for personal conduct from the 1870s.

☞ RULES FOR TEACHERS
— 1872 —

1. Teachers each day will fill lamps, clean chimneys.

2. Each teacher will bring a bucket of water and a scuttle of coal for the day's session.

3. Make your pens carefully. You may whittle nibs to the individual taste of the pupils.

4. Men teachers may take one evening each week for courting purposes, or two evenings a week if they go to church regularly.

5. After ten hours in school, the teachers may spend the remaining time reading the Bible or other good books.

6. Women teachers who marry or engage in unseemly conduct will be dismissed.

7. Every teacher should lay aside from each pay a goodly sum of his earnings for his benefit during his declining years so that he will not become a burden on society.

8. Any teacher who smokes, uses liquor in any form, frequents pool or public halls, or gets shaved in a barber shop will give good reason to suspect his worth, intention, integrity, and honesty.

9. The teacher who performs his labor faithfully and without fault for five years will be given an increase of twenty-five cents per week in his pay, providing the Board of Education approves.

A dedicated teacher works with her students in Live Oak, Texas, in 1887. Such temporary schools were common in the Southwest, especially in Texas and Oklahoma, until a permanent school could be built.

After 1880, teachers were required to pass the eighth-grade graduation tests and become certified. Candidates of "good moral character" could rise through several levels of certification, depending on their years of teaching experience and successful completion of examinations. Teachers also participated in institutes for further training in specific subjects and they began to attend colleges. As recounted in *The West Texas Historical Association Yearbook* (1981), "The country schoolteachers in the first half of this century were the intellectual, social, and often the spiritual leaders of the communities where, until the 1940s, there were no books, few newspapers, and fewer radios."

Teachers also worked with many immigrants, who came to them speaking little or no English. Immigrant children encountered ridicule. When Reuben Goertz, who came from Russia with his parents, attended school in South Dakota, he said, "They were calling us Rooshians, damned Rooshians and

Rooshian peanuts because of the sunflower seeds we all ate." Valentine Vouk described how he and other Slovenian children in Utah mining camps were received in the community: "We had to fight our way to school, and we had to fight our way back." Hispanic Americans faced similar difficulties; as expressed by Salazaar Martinez, who attended a one-room school in Colorado, "They thought because you didn't know the English you were slow in learning." Yet because of the hard work of the children and their country schoolteachers, many states with the largest numbers of immigrants, including Iowa, Kansas, and Nebraska, had the highest literacy rates in the nation.

Around 1880, the teacher at this sod school (far left, with hand on hip) in Thomas County, Kansas, was responsible for twenty-two students ranging from age six to an adult man, who was possibly an immigrant wishing to learn English.

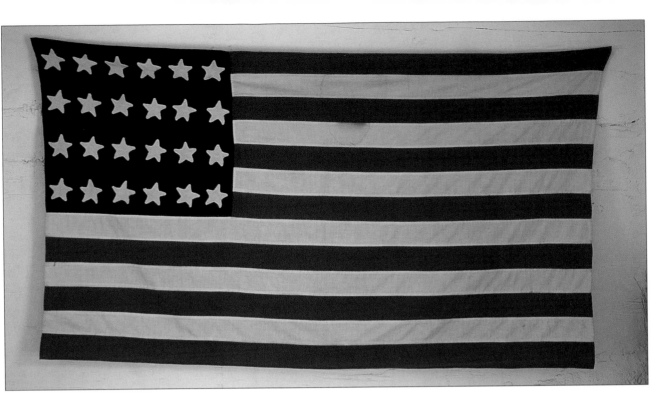

From the woods of the Great Lakes to the mining camps of the Rocky Mountains, teachers helped the children of European immigrants. These children from different countries wanted to speak with each other and English was the common language.

In the South, where African Americans had once been forbidden to learn to read and write, people faced extreme poverty and a lack of adequate schools. Yet as Henry Allen Bullock, the author of *A History of Negro Education in the South*, stated, "It seems that wherever teachers carried their seeds of knowledge, they always found some fertile ground in which to plant them." Similarly, W. E. B. Du Bois fondly recalled his one-room school in *The Souls of Black Folk*, "The schoolhouse was a log hut, where Colonel Wheeler used to shelter his corn. It sat in a lot behind a rail fence and thorn bushes, near the sweetest of springs."

It was said that the teacher made the school, and the proof of success was graduation from the eighth grade, for during that year students had to pass a rigorous comprehensive examination. Held in early June, the graduation ceremony was a major occasion — as important as marriage in the lives of the students. Despite lack of funding and criticism from professional educators, country schools were largely effective in educating rich and poor, Catholic and Protestant, native-born and immigrant.

The schoolhouse was also the primary gathering place for everyone who lived near it. There were no faceless crowds. As one Colorado woman recalled, "the country school was the heart of the community." Public spelldowns were held in the little building, along with other school events at Halloween, Thanksgiving, Christmas, and Easter. Spring and fall programs usually included a box social or pie supper, often held as a fundraiser. There might also be special events for Valentine's Day, Washington's and Lincoln's birthdays, Arbor Day, Memorial Day, Parents' Day, and May Day. "We had a party at the drop of a hat," one man recalled, "and the main place to gather was at the schoolhouse." Everyone rushed home to finish their chores and change into fresh clothes, then they hurried back to the schoolhouse. The end-of-year school picnic

People often picture the little red schoolhouse in a warm, sunny atmosphere. Actually, few schools were red—most weren't even painted until after 1870, when linseed oil and pigment became more economical. Then most were painted white.

included sack races and horseshoe-throwing contests along with recognition of the eighth-grade graduates. Tables groaned under the weight of casseroles, vegetable dishes, and every imaginable recipe for potato salad. There were pickles and preserves from the pantry along with pies, cakes, and cookies. Public meetings, debates, poetry readings, lectures, and music recitals for "personal improvement" also took place in the schoolhouse. Politicians made speeches and people cast ballots in local, state, and national elections in the schoolhouse.

Through the late 1800s, one-room schools were criticized for their shortcomings — underpaid teachers, lack of books, plain buildings, and simple furnishings. In the view of professional educators, the schools were poorly equipped and staffed by young, inexperienced teachers. By the end of the

The one-room school was deeply rooted in the political traditions of the nation. People voted on the school, its location, and its operation. Local, state, and national elections were also held there. Hamlin Garland wrote, "It was a pure democracy."

As part of their morning exercises in 1907, students at Lansing School in New York State raised the American flag. Patriotism assumed even greater importance in country schools after the turn of the century.

1800s, country schools were being pressured to consolidate into larger regional schools. However, many rural people believed that the loss of their school meant the end of their community. They also argued that their students performed as well as—and usually better than—students in better-funded city schools. However, in 1908, President Theodore Roosevelt formed a commission to improve rural life. Its slogan was "Better farming, better business, better living." Out of this program grew a sustained movement to close the one-room schools.

In the early 1900s, one half of all American children attended the 212,000 one-room schools scattered across the land. By 1920, there were 187,948 one-room schools, and through World War II, most rural children still went to one-room schools. After the war, however, consolidation increased as more

The closing of the school sometimes meant the end of a community and its rural heritage. People gathered sadly at auctions to buy the desks, books, maps, globes, and other mementos they and their children—perhaps even their grandchildren—had used.

Iowa cartoonist Bob Artley said of his daily jaunts to school, "There were so many sights and sounds—all part of the ever-changing scene on the prairies that made our walks some of the richest, most memorable times of my childhood."

people moved to the cities. By 1947, the number of one-room schools had plunged to 75,000. So swift was the consolidation that in Illinois, for example, the number of schools was reduced from over 10,000 in 1945 to barely 700 by 1954. Notices offering the public sale of schoolhouses became a common announcement in local newspapers. The growth of cities and suburbs, along with a relentless emphasis upon standardized instruction and consolidation, has nearly wiped out the small country schools of America. Yet it's been a fairly recent change.

Some groups, notably the Amish and the German-speaking Hutterites of eastern South Dakota, continued to send their children to one-room schools or formed their own school districts that exist to this very day. In Pennsylvania alone, 3,000 Amish students attend 100 schools. Although they have attempted to remain separate from the world, over the years Amish children attended one-room schools along with their rural neighbors. When these schools began to consolidate into larger districts, the Amish successfully established their own schools, often purchasing the abandoned buildings that were formerly schools; they have proved to be very competent educators. In the 1950s, they clashed with school officials because of their choice not to formally educate their children beyond eighth grade, believing that there is no need to be educated "over their heads." Teachers are usually single teenage girls who themselves are not educated beyond eighth grade. The Amish believe that small schools located near their homes strengthen a sense of family and community. Amishman Joseph Stoll observed, "The art of teaching, unknown to Amish circles a generation ago, has really caught fire among us."

The Amish believe that they must live "in the world, but not of it." While they emphasize their own closely knit communities, they also interact with the world around them.

Wishing for their children to be educated close to home, the Amish established their own one-room schools in the 1950s. The schools appear no different from the country schools of the past, except that there may also be a horse stable in the yard.

In addition to the Amish, Hutterite, and other parochial schools, there are still more than 800 one-room public schools, mostly in Nebraska and other states on the sprawling plains of the West. There are also one-room schools in the remote mountains of northern New England and on the islands off the coast of Maine, as well as in the state of Washington and scattered villages of Alaska. As in the past, children and teachers in one-room schools confront the uncertainty of the weather. Instead of telephones, teachers may rely on citizens band radios. They also routinely lay in extra supplies of food and water and take survival courses before assuming their duties in the schoolhouse. Teachers sometimes feel isolated and they still lack the best of living accommodations. As one Nevada teacher said, "This trailer is a palace compared with some I've seen." There is also the chronic problem of low pay and the added responsibility of maintaining the school building. Schools are still criticized for the condition of the buildings, lack of equipment, and the limited curriculum. Others argue that students are blessed with remoteness — they don't suffer the tyranny of peer pressure and are allowed to mature as individuals. Teachers in one-room schools insist that their students are independent, confident, and resourceful. Cheryl Carstensen, a teacher at Alfalfa Valley School in South Dakota, says, "I feel that younger and older students learn from each other, not only subject matter but how to give and take. They learn how to work with and cooperate with others, despite vast differences."

In other places, people have come together again to save their one-room schoolhouses. Charming school buildings have begun new lives as museums, town halls, and family homes, as well as businesses and churches. Growstown

Over the course of the nineteenth century the belfry, or bell tower, became a symbol of communities' respect for education. The bells hurried wandering students on their way to school and brought them back when they had drifted off at recess.

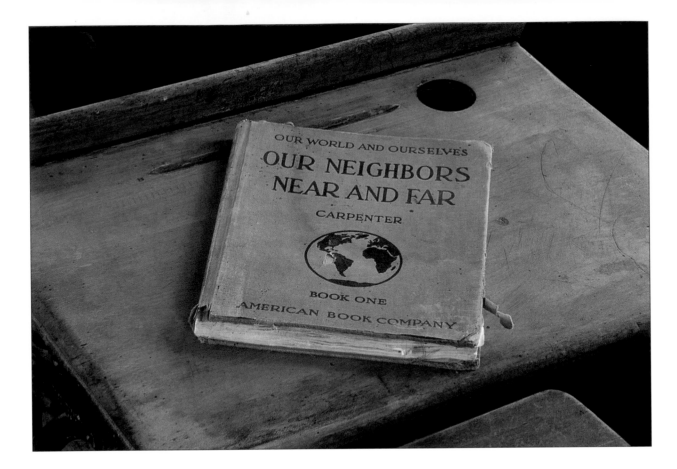

One-room schools were sometimes isolated, overcrowded, and poorly maintained. Frequently, teachers left for better jobs in town. Schools were often stifled by stingy school boards who wouldn't pay to repair leaky roofs or replace old books.

School in Brunswick, Maine, operates a living history museum, complete with a stick-wielding schoolmaster who invites children to learn about education in the past. Ironically, after a century of criticism, it's become apparent that, on the whole, one-room schools did an excellent job. These schools are now widely admired for their sense of community, where a teacher taught students of different ages in a warm, family-like atmosphere. Small and humble, the one-room school was less intimidating than the large fortress-like schools of today.

Many of the "latest" approaches of modern education are actually drawn from traditional methods pioneered in one-room schools. These include small class size, which allows students to progress at their own rate; peer tutoring, in which students help each other; mainstreaming, which permits students with disabilities to attend school with their friends and neighbors; and individual learning centers that encourage small groups of students to work on a variety of subjects. Even the size of classrooms in American schools is based on the dimensions of the one-room school. Although children are now divided into separate grades, the concept of levels based upon academic progress is drawn from one-room schools.

The one-room Eyestone School is maintained by the College of Education at Illinois State University in Normal, Illinois. Today, children visit the school, sit at the wooden desks, and learn about subjects that were taught there in the 1900s.

When she gave up teaching, Laura Ingalls Wilder recalled wistfully, "At the end of the last day of school in March, Laura gathered her books and stacked them neatly on her slate. She looked around the schoolroom for the last time. She would never come back. . . ." (from These Happy Golden Years)

The growth of America as a nation and the education of young people in one-room public schools go hand in hand. For 250 years, the vast majority of children were educated in these schools. Teachers instructed English-speaking children born in the United States as well as wave upon wave of immigrants. Certainly there were some inadequate schools and poor teachers, but bigger schools aren't always the answer either. One educator has suggested that in the "small size and simplicity" of one-room schools, "we might just see something of our future in this remaining part of our past." The quality of education received in most rural schools far exceeded current standards. Most of the one-room schools may now be gone, but over the years, they provided a fine education to millions of Americans, and they still have much to teach us. ◆

Standing in the center of an independent district, the one-room school became a symbol of a shared community life. Like family members, people might fight over the school, but it belonged to everyone, and everyone was keenly interested in it.

FURTHER READING

For those who would like to read more, several books about country or district schools, popularly known as one-room schools, are also available. *America's Country Schools,* by Andrew Gulliford, and *The Old Country School: The Story of Rural Education in the Middle West,* by Wayne E. Fuller, are especially good books. All of the following books, along with *McGuffey's Eclectic Primer* and *McGuffey's First Eclectic Readers* (volumes one through six), were consulted in the preparation of *One-Room School:*

Artley, Bob. *A Country School: Marion No. 7.* Ames, Iowa.: Iowa State University Press, 1989.

Fisher, Sara E. and Stahl, Rachel K. *The Amish School.* Intercourse, Penn.: Good Books, 1986.

Fuller, Wayne E. *The Old Country School: The Story of Rural Education in the Middle West.* Chicago: The University of Chicago Press, 1982.

Fuller, Wayne E. *One-Room Country Schools of the Middle West.* Lawrence, Kans.: University Press of Kansas, 1994.

Gulliford, Andrew. *America's Country Schools.* Washington, D.C.: Preservation Press, 1984.

Hoestetler, John A., ed. *Amish Roots: A Treasury of History, Wisdom, and Lore.* Baltimore, Md.: Johns Hopkins University Press, 1989.

Johnson, Clifton. *Old-Time Schools and School-Books.* Gloucester, Mass.: Peter Smith, 1963. (Originally published by the Macmillan Company in 1904)

Sloane, Eric. *The Little Red Schoolhouse.* Garden City, N.Y.: Doubleday & Co., 1972.

Children may also like to read these books about one-room schools:

Caudill, Rebecca. *Schoolhouse in the Woods*. N.Y.: Holt, Rinehart and Winston, 1949.

Gnagey, Larry. *School Days, School Days, Dear Old Golden Rule Days*. Mahomet, Ill.: Early American Museum, 1996.

Hausherr, Rosemarie. *The One-Room School at Squabble Creek*. N.Y.: Four Winds Press, 1988.

Kalman, Bobbie. *A One-Room School*. N.Y.: Crabtree Publishing Co., 1994.

Lenski, Lois. *Prairie School*. N.Y.: Dell, 1951, 1969.

Tate, Eleanora E. *Front Porch Stories at the One-Room School*. N.Y.: Bantam Books, 1992.

Young readers will also certainly enjoy *By the Shores of Silver Lake, Little Town on the Prairie,* and *Those Happy Golden Years,* which recount Laura Ingalls Wilder's experiences as a student and later as a teacher in a one-room school.

◆

This book is lovingly dedicated to my children
Sarah and Luke, who traveled with me to make photographs
at a number of one-room schools. It was a pure joy to watch
them sit down at the old desks and write on their slates,
imagining themselves deep in the past.

◆

ACKNOWLEDGMENTS

I would like to express my deepest appreciation to the Early American Museum of Mahomet, Illinois, for permission to photograph at their one-room school, and to the following places, where a number of the photographs for this book were made: Bethel School, Friends Creek Conservation District, Argenta, Illinois; Billie Creek Village, Rockville, Indiana; Eyestone School, College of Education, Illinois State University, Normal, Illinois; Lincoln's New Salem, Petersburg, Illinois; Rockome Gardens near Arthur, Illinois; and Weldon Springs State Park, Weldon, Illinois.

I would also like to thank the following organizations for making available a number of wonderful historical photographs for *One-Room School:* DeWitt Historical Society of Tompkins County, Ithaca, New York (pp. 23, 35); Kansas State Historical Society (pp. 8, 9, 18, 31); and Oklahoma State Historical Society (p. 30).

The text of this book is set in 12.5-point Plantin.
Book design by Chris Hammill Paul

Library of Congress Cataloging-in-Publication Data

Bial, Raymond.
    One-room school / Raymond Bial.
        p.   cm.
    Includes bibliographical references.
    Summary: Presents a brief history of the one-room schools that existed in the United States from the 1700s to the 1950s.
    ISBN 0-395-90514-1
    1. Rural schools — United States — History — Juvenile literature. 2. Education, Rural — United States — History — Juvenile literature.
    [1. Schools — History.]   I. Title.
    LC5146.5.B53   1999
    370'.9173'4 — dc21   98-43241   CIP AC

Printed in Singapore

TWP 10 9 8 7 6 5 4 3 2 1